THIS VISION BELONGS TO

_____

Vision Board Kit for Adults
Published by PFM Publishing

© 2020 PFM Publishing

WELCOME TO YOUR BEST YEAR!

A vision board is an inspirational tool used to build a collage of words and pictures that represent your intentions. By collecting your goals and dreams in one space, you can look at them daily to help you reach these goals and reflect on how they are coming true.

This vision board kit is designed to help you choose goals and visualize how to achieve them. The words and pictures are grouped into 8 thematic categories to help you find what you need. Of course, you can use any of the pictures and words in any theme board – it's all up to you!

This kit includes two vision board spreads. Use them to make portable vision boards for you to refer to during the day. You can also use them as "sketchpad" areas to draw ideas for your larger vision boards.

Tips for Choosing Your Vision Board Images

- Goal setting is as much about continually reprioritizing your projects to make small, achievable tasks as it is about finishing all to-do lists. You can achieve a lot of things by breaking them down into smaller actions first.

- Use the words and quotes to reflect your goal or vision for yourself in the future. Consider drawing a rough idea on a scrap sheet of paper. Have fun with your thoughts – sketching can be very inspiring!

- Spend time looking at the pictures to find ones that speak to you.

How to use these Vision Boards

Choose images, words, and pictures that reflect your desired goal or future life. Attach, draw, or paint these pictures and words on the vision board pages. Let your creativity run wild! Imagine your future goal or life as you'd ideally like it to be.

For example, you can use a vision board to visualize where you'd like to be in 1 year or 5 years. Use the words and pictures that illustrate what you'd like to be doing and feeling, where you'd like to be living, etc. You can also use the vision board process to focus on specific areas of your life, like a particular relationship, desired job, or travel destination.

Once you've created your vision for the year or month, refer to it every day. It serves as a reminder of your "roadmap" – you check it daily to make sure you're on track and to remember what you're aiming for. Envisioning your goal will help you prioritize your time to reach that vision.

Happy Visioning!

Getting Started Checklist

To achieve a vision, you also need action

7 steps to guide your vision process:

1. Decide what goal you're really after, and set a clear intention

2. Get all your supplies ready before you begin

3. Make your "creative zone" and atmosphere to get you in the mindset

4. Gather images and words that align with your intention or goal

5. Choose the images and words that resonate with your intention, and paste them

6. Place your vision board where you'll see it daily to visualize your goal

7. Write an "actions" list with steps to help achieve that goal or realize your intention

Example Vision Board

Dream House

Comfortable

My house is full of friends

Vision Board for

Vision Board for _____

New Home

Zen

Redecorate

Creative Zone

Renovate

Dream House

Comfortable

Declutter

Feng Shui

I appreciate my home

I bless my home with love

My house is neat & tidy

All is well in my home

There's no place like home!

There is nothing like staying at home for real comfort.
- Jane Austen

My house is full of friends

I will create my dream home

Date Night

Fun

Enchanting

Magical

Cheerful

Confident

Genuine

Sensitive

Unique

Accepting

Exciting

Magnetic

Sensual

I open my heart to love

I am thankful for my partner

Healthy relationships

FRIENDSHIP IS FOREVER

Happiness begins with me!

Never doubt that I love.
- William Shakespeare, Hamlet

Supportive   Balanced

Exhale negativity

BALANCE

Success

Fulfillment

Hygge

Happy

Learn

Smile

Progress

Ambition

New Skill

Motivated

Focused

Responsibility

Mentor

Strength

I am courageous

I am, and always will be, enough

Enjoy the little things

TAKE A CHANCE!

Focus on your goals

The worst enemy to creativity is self-doubt
- Sylvia Plath

I am worthy

Save wisely   Tenacious

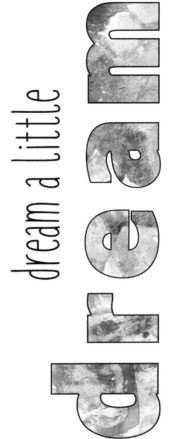

dream a little dream

Knowledge
is
power!

FAMILY

PARTNER

Children

New Baby

Puppy

Little One

Joyful

Maturity

Amazing

Thankful

Playtime

Wife

Husband

Precious

Build

Togetherness

Celebration

I am grateful for my family

I accept my family members

I empower my friends

I AM A GOOD ROLE MODEL!

I am a patient & supportive parent

The family is one of nature's masterpieces
- George Santayana

My children are happy & healthy

Nurture family & friends

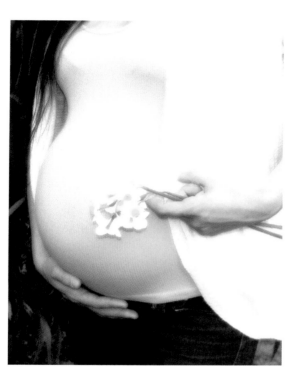

WORK | PROFESSION

PRODUCTIVE Meaning

NEW JOB Proactive

Succeed **Hustle**

Big Goal Creative

Career Change **Exceed**

More Responsibility

Resilient Adapt

Collaborate Lean In

Best Year Ever

I am intelligent & competent

I believe in myself

CHALLENGE = OPPORTUNITY

Achieve your goals

Try again. Fail again. Fail better.
— Samuel Beckett

Lean In   Success Recipe

CARPE DIEM

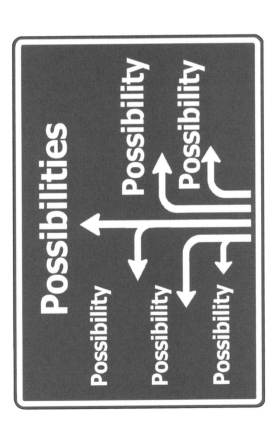

OUTDOORS   Read

STRONG   Music

Cultivate   Explore

Discover   Travel

Dance   Motivate

Yoga   Relax   Teach

Laugh   Create

Spa Day   Leisure Time

I have fun and laugh every day

I enjoy the life I'm living

I am living to my full potential

THIS IS MY YEAR!

Release stress and anxiety

Live with no excuses and travel with no regrets
- Oscar Wilde

Celebrate each goal

LIVE LOUD

WHOLESOME

Biking

ENERGY

Rejuvenation

Daily

Well-being

Marathon

Quality

Natural

Change

Swim Therapy Nourish

Restore

Healing

Uplifting

Healthy

I feel healthy and fit

I will grow my self-esteem

Be Kind to Yourself

KEEP GOING!

Build more confidence

The first wealth is health
- Ralph Waldo Emerson

Change your habits

Relax   Exercise

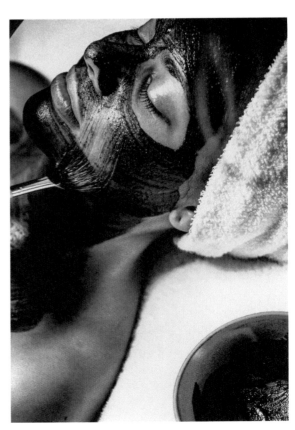

BE HAPPY
BE BRIGHT
BE YOU!

SPIRITUAL

PRAYER Calm Meaning

CENTERED Appreciate

Blessed Inspire

Mindful Peace

Meditation Joyful

God Divine Values

Cultivate Gratitude

Goddess Healthy

Do all things with kindness

I feel connected to the universe

Focus on what matters

BE PRESENT!

I have everything I need

There are always flowers for those who want to see them.
- Henri Matisse

Help Others   Present Moment

Feel Happy & Alive

105

Printed in Great Britain
by Amazon

40724508R00059